WAITING

WAITING

and other poems

JOE WALLER

Otherland Books
2021

Printed in the United States of America. For information, contact Otherland Books online at otherlandbooks.com.

Artwork design by Joe Fontenot, with design input from Joe Waller.

First Otherland Books paperback edition: October 2021
ISBN 978-1-952807-05-3 (paperback)

Published by Otherland Books.
www.OtherlandBooks.com

To Dad,

who took us to bookstores

and let us wander

PREFACE

The story behind this book isn't as clean or as comfortable as I'd like it to be.

When I first started writing, I never really questioned the place writing held in my life. From sharing occasional thoughts on Facebook to writing weekly essays on my blog, I grew used to working with words, and I prided myself (perhaps too much) that I wasn't one of those writers who was so in name only. I actually wrote, eventually producing content on a regular basis. And by God's grace, I saw fruit from the work. In spite of my weaknesses, sins, and slumps, I tried to be faithful to the work, and I think God blessed it.

Poetry fit nicely into the mix, offering a different outlet than prose for thought and expression. Again, as I did the work, I never really questioned it. I was a writer, a poet. I had objective proof to back up those titles. And while I occasionally wondered if I'd ever stop writing on the blog, I assumed I'd still be writing somewhere, that poetry and prose would still hold a prime place in my life. But things change.

As I write these words, it's an overcast day in late May, and I'm realizing these are the first words I've written to be published since late March. And that feels weird to write. In short, 2020 was a difficult year for me, as it was for most people. While the world responded to a global pandemic as well as to tensions and divisions among image bearers near and far, I, like many of you, learned to walk with the Lord while feeling isolated and distant from others. I was also walking through a season of confusion and pain on a personal level as I struggled to discern the Lord's will for my life, and even now, that season hasn't ended. In the last year and a half, I've felt more tension, more disorientation, more distance, more hurt, more shame, and more fear than I can ever remember feeling before now. The Lord has been exposing sin I don't want to acknowledge, calling for trust I don't want to give, and working for change I'm afraid to accept. But he's been faithful through it all, giving mercy for my missteps and grace sufficient for the day. I'm not where I want to be, but I'm learning to listen, learning to wait, and learning to walk by faith.

These poems reflect a bit of that journey. Like the first book (*As I Learn to Walk*, 2018), this one collects poems from the blog, picking up after the last poems of the first book and continuing through the end of 2020. Because of the context in which they were written, I'm afraid they may reflect more of a struggle of faith than a settled spirit. There may be more darkness than light in these pages. But I hope you see that the light isn't absent. I hope you see that the questions are raised in recognition that there exists one who can answer, that griefs are expressed in the hope that the comforter will do his work. I'm more broken than I want to admit; the Lord is more sufficient than I yet know. So I offer these words in hope that they serve you in the journey. May the Lord meet you in your working, meet you in your playing, meet you in your resting, and meet you in your waiting.

To the praise of his glory,
Joe Waller

- POEMS -

Rest

Rest.
Reminded of mortality,
Rest.
Refocus on eternity.
Rest.
Refresh your soul's vitality.
Rest.

Deception

Beware the traps of trappings.
Beware the lies of looks.
Appearances may not reflect the heart.
'Neath many modest wrappings
Lie hearts ensnared by hooks.
Deception is a most devilish art.

The Plagiarists

To take a thought, original and good,
And claim it as one's own thought, own design;
To see another's work and call it, "Mine,"
Accepting honor as the author should;
To speak until the people understood
The thief to be the writer of each line,
Scratching the author's name off from the spine
Till truth's uncov'ring be no likelihood—
Delusion tempts souls to these actions take,
Tries to erase the author, take his place.
And do we not each make this fatal nod?
The author still is living and awake,
Yet we would rob his glory, slight his face.
Have we not all been plagiarists of God?

Keep Running

Keep running.
Pain oft will come, will not relent.
Keep running.
You may well feel your strength is spent.
Keep running.
Pour out to God all your lament.
Keep running.

Keep running.
Lay down all weight. Let go all sin.
Keep running.
Temptation comes. Refocus, then
Keep running.
And when you stumble, rise again.
Keep running.

Keep running
Pleasures of life will bid you stay.
Keep running.
Stay focused on the narrow way.
Keep running.
Pass through the night to brightest day.
Keep running.

Commonplace

God of burning bushes, smoking mountains,
Clouds and flaming pillars in the distance,
God who spoke the earth into existence,
Calling from dry rocks fresh, flowing fountains,
Are you just as present in the present,
In the average and ordinary?
Does your presence with us ever vary
If our days are boring or unpleasant?
For, it seems, our lives are unexciting,
Work and worship in a world of faces—
Seems so commonplace, these common places.
Is it true, O God, you are inviting
Those with ears to hear to live in wonder?
In our silence, might we hear your thunder?

Steady

Wait for him, my soul,
Overwhelmed though you may be.
Trust him when you cannot see.
He is in control.
This will play a role.
Though you long to fight or flee,
Still your heart and bend your knee.
He will make you whole.

Walking

When roads diverge, how are we then to choose
The good, acceptable, and perfect way?
We guess what we might gain, what we might lose,
But which is better cannot ever say.

We walk by faith. Indeed. But does that mean
That we distrust our wisdom and our eyes?
Should we step forth in spite of what we see,
Ignoring earth whilst looking to the skies?

Or, in our ignorance, would it be best
To stop, be still, and know that you are God?
To proceed not with hastiness but rest,
To trust you to make straight the roads we trod?

Lord, in our walking, let our focus be
Not as much on our paths as upon thee.

Center

Keep me from distraction from whimsy and woe.
Let me be fixed always on you,
To trust when you lead where I wish not to go
And trust when you lead where I do.

The Deceiver

Subtle are the seeds you sow, deceiver,
Passive possessor quietly at work
At shifting my soul's focus till I shirk
Habits that distinguish a believer
For old futilities. You water waste
To fill the garden grounds with thorns and weeds.
In fear, I grow impatient, turn to haste.
Forgetting faith, I fall. Temptation feeds
Upon my flesh's efforts. Travesty
Becomes me in the mire of my pursuit
When I forget my strength comes from the root
Of David, from a higher majesty
Than your false throne can feign. I will endure.
Though you assail, my advocate is sure.

Reform

I do not trust my heart,
These feelings, these desires,
For though they, at the start,
Resemble warming fires,
They turn to fun'ral pyres.
So teach me to aspire
For your refining fire,
And, for your glory, start
My t'ward a pure desire,
One after your own heart.

A Prayer to Lead

Their eyes now look to me.
I wonder what they see.
Do they detect the doubts and fears,
Perceive the weights, the hidden tears?
Or do they only see
A car'cature of me:
A man of wisdom, love, and care,
Firm in the faith and full of pray'r?
Lord, if they look to me,
Let me e'er look to thee.
Be evident in all I do
That they, through me, better see you.
Let me be all for thee,
More you and less of me,
A servant serving all around
That they in love would e'er abound.

The Pharaoh

In water did this story start,
In water did it end;
And water now reminds my heart
Of all the ways I sinned.

My brother-enemy arrived,
A gift born from the Nile.
Where others perished, he survived,
Vital'ty from the vile.
He learned our ways but kept his kin
Within his heart and will.
Seeing "injustice" 'mongst his men,
He chose to act, to kill.
In fear he fled (I knew not where).
I thought him lost for good.
Then he returned with greying hair
And with a staff of wood.
"Freedom to worship" was his cry,
Presumpt'ous his request.
"Increase the work" was my reply,
And put his god to test.
Then came the signs, small at the first,
Then day by day they grew.

From blood to dark to death, the worst
Came to my home. I knew
My gods had each been overruled,
Their promises proved wrong.
I knew in them we had been fooled
When mourning was our song.
So I relented and released
The captives to the wild.
The land had rest. The plagues then ceased.
My reign had been defiled.
And so I brooded, plotted, chose
To turn around my loss,
And with a burning vengeance, rose
To catch before their cross.
And there I found them, easy prey,
Defenseless 'gainst my might,
And I beheld his god that day
Work wonders in my sight.
Now all is lost. Now I depart.
My wisdom I rescind.
In water did his story start.
In water did mine end.

Building

Unless you build the house, my Lord,
I work to build in vain.
Unless I use your brick and board,
I will not last the rain.
Let me assemble by your sword,
That, in my life till gain,
My work will ever work toward
Eternal life's refrain.

Nebuchadnezzar

Behold the beast king, the once-man who was
Once full of reason, robed in royal hues,
Wretched and ragged now, soaked by the dews
Of seven seasons. Behold him who does
Not remember the ways of his fathers,
Driven to dwell with the beasts at the word
Of him who rules over human and bird,
Over kingdoms and rulers and bothers.
Behold the beast king, his reason restored,
More human now than e'er he was. He sees
That he is but a steward of decrees,
Humbly admitting he cannot afford
With all his wealth the cost of arrogance.
The king learned his own need for reverence.

A Prayer for Fear

Let us behold as much of you as we
May bear with eyes still tethered to this age,
And purify our vision till we see
You in the printed ink upon the page.
Let us see past the threats and throes of life,
Past ev'ry disappointment, ev'ry loss.
Let us see sov'reignty midst earthly strife
And find our comfort in the crimson cross.
And let us lay before you our dismay,
Discouragement, and disillusionment.
And let us ponder worthily and pray
And work out our salvation and repent.
Let trembling be our lot through joys and tears,
For true fear swallows up all lesser fears.

Weather

The rain one day will end.
The broken skies will mend.
Hope then in he who maketh all things new.
For though your heart may rend,
His presence doth transcend
All storms of life, and he will see you through.

Christ Above

Christ above my heart's desire.
Christ above my timing.
Christ above all I aspire.
Christ above my rhyming.
Christ above my greatest fears.
Christ above all pleasures.
Christ above my future years.
Christ above all treasures.
Christ above my past mistakes.
Christ above my glory.
Christ above all earthly aches.
Christ above my story.
Christ above all toil and strife.
Christ above whatever.
Christ above this fleeting life
Now and to forever.

Thanksgiving

You give us the ability to give,
For all we have to give, in truth, is yours.
The very breath we breathe, the days we live,
Our daily bread—each comes from heaven's stores.
Lord, let us not forget that all is grace,
That we have earned not one of all our joys,
And let us fix our eyes upon your face
Above all earthly troubles, tasks, and toys.
Forgive us when we want more than your love,
And fit us to receive and be content.
Yours is the universe and all thereof.
The proof of your provision is Advent.
In thanks, we rest and look toward the Son,
Dependent on the independent one.

Satisfy

Nothing here will satisfy me.
Still, these treasures tempt me, try me.
Trust in them will truly guide me
Straight into the grave.
Only you can satisfy me.
Perfect Father, purify me.
Set me free and ever guide me.
Only you can save.

Advent

The proem to the poem of humanity
Was set against the backdrop of captivity,
Was cast with souls encumbered by profanity,
Was opened not with pomp but with nativity.
The word, the light, the lion-lamb, the majesty
Of heaven, holiness in his humility,
Appeared in righteousness to end the amnesty
And fix final salvation from futility.

The method of his advent seemed absurdity
To those who thought they knew the king's priority,
Yet as the virgin held mortal eternity,
The world beheld the hope of our infirmity.

And all the damned ones shuddered as the surety
Of justice came in love to face depravity,
To bear the curse of sin and give security
That God shall satisfy creation's cavity.
So hope. His coming heralds a community
Where sin will not be suffered—there immunity
From falling from his presence. Perfect unity
Of love will lead to worship of triunity.

Savior

Crying infant.
Newborn king.
Holy instant.
Offering.
Promised mercy.
Perfect grace.
Blessed story.
Heaven's face.

Two Carpenters

The wood was rough, but it would serve him well.
He chose it not for elegance or style
But for its faithfulness. A little while
(And, too, a little work) and he could sell
It with a workman's pride. And he could tell,
Though now it lay unstructured in a pile,
That with some nails, a hammer, and a file,
His work would not be broken though it fell.

Its strength would bear its strength one dark noel
(The first of all). And in its content's smile
Was love born now to one day reconcile
On other wood, the darkness to dispel.
His parents smiled as into sleep he fell.
The wood was rough, but it would serve him well.

The Recurring Frustration

I want to read but cannot find the time.
Responsibilities fill ev'ry day
With tasks and cares I dare not cast away,
And reading, sadly, can't always be prime.
And on the rare occasions when the time
Presents itself with freedom to peruse
A poem or a chapter (which to choose?)
Uninterrupted (oh the joy sublime!),
I find my eyes work only for a time
Before I catch myself rereading lines
While heavy eyelids cover eyes that pine
After the peaks I've grown too tired to climb.
So words within my reach remain unread
As I desire books not so much as bed.

The Moment

The moment passes, same as all the rest,
Save for an added weight, a seeming force.
Some see in it the ending of a test.
Some find in it the start of a new course.
We hope to lay aside all that is past
And welcome future's possibilities.
We hope to make a change and make it last.
We often miss the forest for the trees.
For ev'ry day behind has led to now,
The good and bad both mingled in the soul.
Experience informs our present plod.
Find hope not in a momentary vow
But in the one who truly holds control.
Entrust this and all moments to your God.

By Faith

I feel the pain but cannot find the benefit.
The path I would have chosen seemed a better fit.
Yet tests portend the sacrifice. I see my wraith
Point to my cross and call me to walk forth by faith.
Faith does not promise answers, bids me follow still;
Points past my understanding to the Father's will;
Grounds hope not in the knowing but in being known;
Endures uncertainty certain of heaven's throne.
Faith fixes focus not on the ephemeral
But finds eternal joy within the temporal.
It lays aside success and loss for higher gain
And trusts the one who gives and takes to justly reign.
Obedience bids me to die to self in this,
To trust the process in this brief parenthesis.
The work you do is good, as it shall always be.
Steadfast unto perfection is the course for me.

The Call

Count the cost before you follow me.
I require more than you now foresee.
Would you seize this joyful slavery,
Or do you prefer captivity?

Give Me a Love for People

Give me a love for people,
For runny noses and achy heads,
For homesick widows with empty beds,
For orphaned children who long for homes,
For refugees on a strange sea's foams,
For unwashed sweaters and hole-filled shoes,
For ears weary with unhappy news,
For feeble bodies both young and old,
For hearts white-hot and for hearts now cold,
For neighbors nearby and far away,
For friends who go and for friends who stay,
For enemies who have not earned peace,
For captives awaiting their release,
For those who share my blood and my name,
For names I would prefer not to claim,
For fallen minds that think much like me,
For souls with whom I still disagree,
For happy voices singing their songs,
For those I fear because of their wrongs,
For tongues I do not now understand,
For both innocent and guilty hands,
For those remembered, those forgotten,
For both highborn and misbegotten,

For image bearers in ev'ry form,
For the lost, the fervent, the lukewarm.
Give me a love for people.

Christians

We are living sacrifices
Still allowed to scream;
Not left to our own devices,
Still inspired to dream;
Free to choose in daily choices,
Held by sov'reignty;
Speaking with our mortal voices
Of eternity.

Hope Well

Hope. But hope well, fixed in this conviction,
Fixed within the grasp that cannot falter.
Grasp the truth, this holy benediction:
Holy hope will meet you at the altar.

God With Us

E'er expanding space cannot contain you.
There you stand with flesh and blood and sinew.

Little Windows

Little windows show us shocking visions,
Tempt us to expect what is not fitting,
Make into our minds subtle incisions,
May be slyly twisting and remitting
Our convictions. Still, we give attention.
Still, we turn away from concentration.
Still, we stoop to savage condescension.
Still, we step into the conflagration.
Portals to such vast opportunities
May, in truth, be endless winding hallways.
Consider steps in these communities.
Keep perspective. Know that there is always
More to life than windows ever show us,
More to lose than windows ever show us.

From Bossier to New Orleans

Down the forty-nine to ten we travel.
Feasts of kings and cakes, our destination.
Down we go, our worries to unravel.
Food and fellowship, our motivation.
Past the city's lights and steel magnolias.
Past the airbase and the coliseum.
Past the capital after Angola.
Past the lakes and rivers and museums.
Standing still, undrowned through stormy seasons,
History endures through celebration.
All Louisiana knows her treasure.
So we travel for our varied reasons—
Stories, memories, anticipation—
Seeking carnival in greater measure.

Bitterness

Bitterness inhabits me,
Burns within these weary bones,
Breaks the heart's song, shifts the key—
Melodies to monotones.

Feelings fixate on frustrations,
Fast forgetting joy and peace.
Anger turns to accusations
As emotions seek release.

Father, temper this, my temper,
Tossed midst waves of woes and whims.
Devastate my vile distemper.
Heal my heart through holy hymns.

Christ has borne more suffering,
Bears me up in all I face.
Make of me an offering.
Let me ever sing of grace.

Words

Our words divide. They rend each other's souls.
The Word rends our division, offers peace
To war-torn hearts that long for true release
From slavery, from talk's eternal tolls.
Our words deceive. They prove our father well.
The Word destroys deception in his wake
And takes e'en death's ability to take
That souls may surely hope to 'scape from hell.
Our words decay. They cannot help but fade.
The Word will never not be, shall endure
Should sea and sky be shaken. He is sure,
Salvation for the burdened and afraid.
Lord, teach our tongues, if e'er we speak, to be
Tamed by the Truth, to ever echo thee.

The Light Burden

The lofty halt. The lowly enter in.
The pious scoff. The poor are born again.
The strong still work. The weak embrace his rest.
The wise stay blind. The blind see and are blessed.

All Things Work for the Good, You Say

All things work for the good, you say.
I do not doubt the truth.
But shall I see the good one day,
Ever detect your better way
When circumstances ever lay
Before my doubtful heart a "may"
Which shakes the faith of youth
With fears I shudder to convey?

My mind is prone to wonder, though
I know you to be wise.
When progress on the road is slow,
When seasons threaten me with snow
Or desert heat, when all is woe—
God, how much further must I go?
My limits are my eyes.
I cannot see how I must grow.

Yet none can know your mind. You see
Past ev'ry fear I face.
So when I lose perspective, be
The peace amidst confusion, he

Whose presence makes the raging sea
A place of rest: tranquility
Of soul because of grace,
Enduring to eternity.

Fiction

Untrue stories still can teach us
Truths which shape our living stories.
Fiction's mirror still may reach us
With eternal glories.

All reality is brimming
With more truth than can be spoken.
Still, too many minds are dimming.
Let yours be awoken.

All To Your Throne

Let me be part of your story unfolding.
Make me remember I am not my own.
Batter my heart till, your glory beholding,
I defer all to your throne.

I Do Not Want to Follow You Today

I do not want to follow you today,
And though I know the path you set is right,
I do not want to walk the narrow way.

I struggle now to find the words to say
That, though I do not want to leave the light,
I do not want to follow you today.

I still will read the Bible, still will pray;
Yet as I stand before the darkest night,
I do not want to walk the narrow way.

God, can I still within your purpose stay
When, as emotions fill my soul with fright,
I do not want to follow you today?

Storm clouds have come and turned clear skies to grey.
God, must I walk by faith and not by sight?
I do not want to walk the narrow way.

These few concerns before your throne I lay.
Lord, leave me not, though, in this temp'ral plight,
I do not want to follow you today,
I do not want to walk the narrow way.

Empty

Empty is the tomb.
Empty are its threats.
Curse borne from the womb
Cancelled with our debts.
Freedom from our doom
Found in heaven's nets.

I'm afraid of the prayer I just prayed

I'm afraid of the prayer I just prayed.
I'm afraid that you might answer it.
But I'm also afraid of this season I'm in.
And you're here with me now, and you'll be with me then.
And I know, one day, I'll get through it
And be thankful for prayers that I prayed.

When Doubts and Fears Assail

There are truths I know yet struggle to believe.
You know all my struggles, yet you never leave.

Proverbs 1

My boy, beware the moral poverty
Of those intent on feeding discontent.
The end of all their labor is lament.
They die in lust for blood and property.
Remain not an antagonist to truth
Nor love the follies of your fallen state.
You need not face the unrepentant's fate,
For wisdom offers hope to humble youth.
Know well that you will never know as well
As he who rules reality with love,
So hallow him and turn a list'ning ear.
Invite instruction and commit to dwell
At wisdom's fountainhead. Heed God above
And rest within a state of holy fear.

Another Prayer for Faith

When bothered, I am often prone to blither
About how I must work, my faith to prove.
A mustard seed's supply of faith can weather.
I scarce can muster e'en a trace thereof.

I do not wish to see the fig tree wither.
I do not long to make the mountain move.
But I desire today a shorter tether.
Lord, help my unbelief and lack of love.

The Secret

Contentment is not found within a lack
Of ev'ry good and perfect gift bestowed,
For some with no possessions answer back,
Embittered by what ne'er to them was owed.

Contentment is not found in much excess,
In temp'ral pleasures, comforts of this earth,
For some see all their wealth as somehow less
Than adequate to validate their worth.

The secret lies not in the circumstance
But in the hope held by the seeking soul.
Events tempt t'ward despair or bid us dance.
In both extremes, the Lord retains control.

Nothing in history has e'er sufficed
To satisfy our souls save only Christ.

A Prayer to Abide

I want to walk with hope though there be sadness.
I want to be at peace though there be war.
I want to remain sober in the madness.
I want to trust, not knowing what's in store.
I want my life to testify to blessings
Surpassing the self-pity that I feel.
I want to stand in spite of second-guessings.
I want my love to be alive and real.
I want my joy to show through circumstances,
Joy found not in my circumstance or sight.
I want my setbacks to serve your advances,
That, in the darkness, I reflect your light.

Sights

I am afraid of silly stuff
I know to be not true.
I show my faith is largely fluff
When tests begin anew.
All fear that you are not enough
Stems from a faulty view.
When calm sea waters become rough,
I take my eyes off you.

The Means and the End

True, hopes deferred may make hearts sick,
But so may hopes fulfilled.
And comfort for a smold'ring wick
May not be what it willed.
For often hopes transfix upon
The means and so detach
The running from the marathon,
The sewing from the patch.
And what was meant to foster growth
In fear and love of God
Becomes instead a broken oath
Upon the paths we trod.
Tis better far to see the gifts
In light of he who gives
Lest graces be turned into rifts,
Nouns turned to adjectives.
Remember heaven ne'er forgets
Its own. God e'er shall be
Sure hope in spite of fears and frets,
The anchor in the sea.

Its Full Effect

O clarifying lack of clarity,
O beauty of this brief bewilderment,
O need that drives me to the firmament,
Grow faith in unfamiliarity.
Let suff'ring sear my sin but not my soul,
The stone-turned-flesh be softened by the flame
And purified of all not for the name,
That what is partial now would be made whole.
Endurance marks the path to character,
And character to unashamed hope,
Sure of the unseen God by his seen grace.
We know in part, see but a car'cature
Till faith's perspective (holy periscope)
Becomes our sight and we see face to face.

Faithful

Grant me the strength to do what honors you,
And let me ever be
A testament to what your grace can do.

Let ev'ry word I speak be pure and true
So others hear and see
My what, why, when, and how point to a who.

Shape the affections of this heart made new
And make them more like he
Who gave his life to rescue and renew.

God, teach my mind to never misconstrue
What you require of me,
To count the cost and see the journey through.

And let me be found faithful to the two-
Fold sum of your decree,
That love might be my story's overview.

Limits

I cannot do it all today.
I cannot do it all.
In spite of what I think or say,
I still will fail and fall.
But time will ever slip away,
And stress will foster disarray,
And so I cannot help but pray,
For I am very small.
Yet in my weakness, you display
Your holy wherewithal
To keep me on the narrow way.

But Who Am I To Thee?

I am a novelty to most,
A treasure to but two or three,
One face amidst history's host,
But who am I to thee?

I am an upright man to most,
A sinner to but two or three,
One saint amidst the sacred host,
But who am I to thee?

I am unworthy, more than most,
A traitor to the one-in-three,
One soul amidst a sinful host.
Oh, who am I to thee?

I am a son because the most
August of sons rose morning three
With freedom for the captive host,
For he was truly thee.

I am yours to the uttermost,
A slave no more to two or three,
One voice—known—singing with your host.
E'er more am I to thee.

Perspective and Provision

Frustrated by my failure to perceive
The movement of the invisible one
Whose work, though purposeful, leaves me undone
Till no one save the Savior can relieve
The longing my soul feels to find its home.
I both believe and struggle to believe
That hope endures because of heaven's Son,
That fears will fade, that victory is won;
And in this moment, I cannot conceive
How this cross leads beyond a catacomb.
I see I am shortsighted, prone to think
No sign of water means no future drink.
Such circumstances hold a hollow taunt.
God is my shepherd. I shall never want.

Still

Be still, and still be creature.
He still knows ev'ry feature of your soul.
Time is a trying teacher,
But tender is the one still in control.

Bear Up

I know that he is good but do not know
What form his goodness in this time will take.
My sight is bound by barriers below.
I cannot feel the healing in the break.

Bear up, my soul. Remember all the ways
He proved his faithfulness in ev'ry test.
You do not need to see beyond the haze
In order to partake in perfect rest.

Beatitude

He knows that you are weary.
He hears each cry and query of his own.
The battered and the bleary
Are blessed. They will behold their father's throne.

Despite What Eyes Can See

I neither like nor understand your "no,"
Yet neither are required for me to trust
That you make straight the way I am to go
E'en when desires give way to thirst and dust.
If you withhold no good thing from your own,
Then your withholding must be for the best.
I may feel I am utterly alone;
I know you have a purpose for this test.
The LORD will never fail. Thus it is joy
To walk the path of sorrow for a time.
The surest hope, none ever can destroy.
No valley deep can halt the upward climb.
Your love holds fast despite what eyes can see,
Thus sight always defers to faith in thee.

Posture of Worship

Palms outstretched in offering,
Bowing low, I meet my king.
In humility, I sing.

In the market, in the square,
Souls surround me. You are there.
Though I move, you hear my prayer.

In the darkness cold and still,
As I sit against my will,
I look up, and you fulfill.

Through the music and the word,
Worship serves to undergird.
I receive, and I am heard.

May my posture ever be
Tempered by eternity
As I learn to walk with thee.

Wants

We want but are not satisfied in gain,
And so we gain new wants to add to old.
This futile journey is an old refrain,
Of wants too weak to trust the Story told.
"Our hearts are restless till they rest in thee,"
The saint once wrote, and still his words resound.
They ring from Africa across the sea,
True both on foreign and familiar ground.
For we were wrought to reckon with our ends,
To know the purpose t'ward which passion points:
Temp'ral desires call for that which transcends;
What leads to life divides marrow and joints.
O LORD, align our wanting with your will,
And turn our hearts to you and so fulfill.

The Pen

You have been used to chronicle the rise
And fall of kingdoms, showing them to be
Far frailer than what many then could see.
You lend perspective to our searching eyes,
Reminding us that, under younger skies,
Stories of fears and foes and fantasy
Appeared in fiction and biography.
You keep the record of both truth and lies.

And through mere momentary markings, you
Can capture glimpses of eternity,
Can testify to what is ever true
In ev'ry ebb and flow of history,
Can tell the tale of what one Word can do
When written in the heart of one like me.

The Character of Contentment

To be where one is present with no thought
For how one might escape the present state.
To hold that one is held when one feels caught.
To feel the urge to run, yet still to wait.
To know that his provision is enough,
His grace sufficient for the task at hand.
To recognize the road indeed is rough
And follow still with faith in his command.
To seek his reign and righteousness above
The chasing of all momentary needs.
To trust that ev'ry test is ruled by love.
In darkest valleys, still the Shepherd leads.
From worry and comparison refrain;
His sov'reignty and purposes remain.

A Prayer for Sanctification

Please help me, LORD, to pass this test,
To wait within this purging flame
In faith that you know what will best
Exalt your holy name.

Correct all misdirection of
My wants until my will fits thine,
My soul steeped long in faith and love,
A branch bound to the vine.

The Process

Haunted by the fear of what comes after
That hard resignation of all hoping
In all plans of mine, the feeble groping
For a road that will not warrant laughter.
Rip a wall down and remove a rafter—
So it feels when dreams begin to crumble.
"All is lost!"—the thought when you but stumble.
Can we lose and not despair thereafter?

Faith and patience: bittersweet but proven.
Bitter for they bid us leave our hiding
In the safety of our sight and timing.
Sweet for we, though limited, yet move in
Sov'reignty's provision, e'er abiding
In his goodness, t'ward him ever climbing.

The Smile

There was a smile for years within the shadows.
I saw no eyes but knew it smiled at me.
It wore a glee like one who watched the gallows
To revel in death and depravity.
I lived for years in fear of its abuses;
Its haunting was oppressive in its scope.
It laughed at my defenses and excuses
And steadily eroded all my hope.
How can one contradict a stronger power?
How can one run from what cannot be found?
I felt its gaze upon me ev'ry hour
And knew it laughed e'en when it made no sound.
But something changed the day that I surrendered
And ceased to fear the smile to fear the crown.
I turned from dark to light, life was engendered,
And what once smiled at me began to frown.

Fall

The cold has come, the darkness steals the day,
But not in ev'ry way.
For still some voices sing
Of home, a land untouched by this decay.
Though presently we feel a bitter sting
Of this scene's disarray,
For those who know the King,
The final act is not the fall, but spring.

Joy

Joy to all the world, to ev'ry creature.
God has come to dwell with his creation.
He who knows us—ev'ry fallen feature—
Put an end to our great separation.
Now his presence leads to our rejoicing
For he turns our mourning into dancing.
In the depths of darkness, we are voicing
Victory: the kingdom is advancing.
Joy now grows in souls steeped in the Spirit,
Joy still true when trials stand before us.
Steadfast, nothing e'er can steal or smear it.
It now fuels the everlasting chorus.
On our journeys, this is holy leaven.
We are strengthened by the joy of heaven.

Saved

"Do not fear me," spoke the specter,
And I was afraid.
Death would surely follow from this brush.
But the holy soul collector,
With his wounds displayed,
Welcomed me and did the devil crush.

Faith

To lose the world,
To gain one's soul,
With sail unfurled,
Release control
And trust the wind
To bring you to the end.

The Shining of Light

Now light has broken through the shroud of darkness.
The dark shall not prevail,
For he does not and will not ever fail.
His love holds fast in spite of our heart's hardness.
He heard our hopeless wail
And cured our state with his own cross and nail.

Provision

If you, LORD, withhold no good thing,
I must believe this present sting
Is evidence of providence,
A chance to give an offering.
My hopes and plans I humbly bring,
Releasing all, surrendering
To better sense your immanence
Within the shadow of your wing.

Through the Cold

Cold, crisp air, bright lights, fresh holly
Mingle joy and melancholy.
In this season, saints are jolly
And still cold.

Friendly faces full of laughter
Offer hope. But what comes after?
Garnished rooftops hide a rafter
Bare and cold.

All the best of man's adorning
May well hide a heart in mourning.
Sorrow rarely gives forewarning
Of its cold.

But this chapter of the story
Is, for him, known territory.
This is still the road to glory,
Long and cold.

Christmas came and comes each season,
A reminder of the reason
Hope endures in spite of treason,
Through the cold.

At the End

How many little moments will we find
Were not without significance at all
But were the subtle graces of a kind
Untarnished by the twisting of the fall?
How many hours of testing will reveal
Themselves to be the reasons for our joys?
How many wounds will show they served to heal?
How many pains upset the serpent's ploys?
How many seasons thought to have no end
Did end one day with mercy fresh and new?
How many things seemed only offend
But deepened both my love and faith in you?
How often is there more than eyes can see?
How little do we understand of thee.

Growing

Refining is taking place.
Desires, not weeds, just not yet in full bloom,
push through the dry dirt only to be pruned
by the one gardener who never errs.
There is loss, but there is growth,
strength from the stripping,
life from death.
The breath I struggle to catch remains his,
sufficient,
efficient
for the work, the fruit, he desires.

The Test

Each present heartache seems to be the worst.
Each test of faith feels fiercer than the last.
Unfounded fears lie shattered in the past,
Yet fear still strikes with strength as at the first.
You start to wonder if you might be cursed
To never have the faith of the steadfast.
You long for constancy but e'er contrast
Your faith with fear, fulfillment with more thirst.
Perhaps the moment's pain does not intrude
Except to prove the possibility
Of suffering to serve a higher end.
The path of faithfulness does not preclude
The faltering and fallibility
But uses these to lead you to a friend.

Bittersweet

Knowing God is growing you, refining
Faith in faithfulness, slowly aligning
Heart and head and habit with his beauty.
Deeming discipline a joyful duty.
Knowing too his work is far from finished,
That you are yet still must be diminished,
That the recognition of a reason
May not mark the closing of the season.

Weakness

I do not want this weakness anymore,
This want of strength, this will so rife with lack.
I tire of always falling further back,
Forgetting truths I knew just days before.
Corruption keeps its hold upon my core,
Each fault of mine another little crack,
Each inability a grave attack
In this, the never-ending inner war.
But at the end of my ability,
Your grace, sufficient for my ev'ry need,
Reminds me of the testifying host
Of those who grasp their own futility
And trust instead *your* ev'ry word and deed,
So trials become their joy, the cross their boast.

A Prayer for Reform

I know I ought to be in awe of you,
To walk in holy fear,
For you are far and you are near,
Both present and surpassing all I know.
But as I go,
I often show
Ambivalence or apathy and throw
My heart to fleeting treasures here.
Reform my faith this year
And fill my soul with love for what is true.

A Prayer During a Pandemic

Death's shadow looms o'er us, but we fear not,
For with us walks the life, the light, of men,
Sov'reign o'er ev'ry plague, problem, and plot,
Perfect in power, faithful yet again.
You have been with us, will be with us still,
Though days be long and lonely in the land.
We feel the curse. So many are so ill.
God, this is not the future we had planned.
But you are e'er at work, and so we wait.
And we believe (but help our unbelief).
Let faith grow more than worry for our fate.
Let worship be our joy and our relief.
O Lord, you give. O Lord, you take away.
O let your name be blessed by us this day.

Sadness

My throat grows tight as speech begins to falter.
I work in words but fight to share them now.
Why do things have to change?
My heart burns as I call to mind the Psalter.
Another break is teaching me to bow.
It strikes me now as strange:
Saved twenty years, and still I fear the altar.
I play the victim though I made the vow.
My feelings rearrange.
Grant me the faith to trust your hand to alter
What I desired and planned, and show me how
To praise in the exchange.

It Came To Pass

It came to pass:
A simple phrase
So full of hope.

The seasons change.
What now is wrong
Will be made right.

Like flow'rs and grass
Are fearful days
And daunting slopes.

Think it not strange
When night seems long.
Soon comes the light.

A Lament

I cannot find the words to share my grief.
I sit instead in silence, and I mourn
Those dreams that were conceived but never born.
I pray for rest, for respite, for relief.
Remind me of the gospel's grand motif:
Light for the lost and hope for the forlorn.
This all is grace, the flower and the thorn.
Lord, I believe, but help my unbelief.
I am a broken soul haunted by fears
With naught to offer but these feeble prayers
For hope and help to trust you through the tears.
With glory soon revealed, no pain compares,
So I cling now to you, the God who hears.
O Father, comfort me in these affairs.

Monday Evening

Potatoes baking in the oven.
The smell—oil and earth commingled—
seasons the air, circulated
by the unit's fan, its white noise drowning
the quiet, though the quiet is still felt.
I am alone here.
I recall the doctrines, that you
are ever present, ever with me.
Why then can I not feel you,
hear you, smell you, detect you
somehow in the room?
The silence seems stronger sometimes.
But truth is truth, even when
perception challenges reality.

Endure

Lost and wounded, weary, worn.
Not forgotten. Not forlorn.
In the breaking, hope is born
Fresh and new.

Feeling shattered. Feeling shorn.
Stretched past limits; still untorn.
Mercy meets the ones who mourn
Like the dew.

Healing

I have watched this wound heal for a week or so.
Day to day, I do not detect
movement of skin,
change of shape,
decrease of pain.
Then one day, I do.
The gap is less wide, the depth less deep.
All around,
dead skin darkens,
new skin appears.
It is not finished. It is still sore.
I wanted the process to be faster.
Nevertheless, the process is working.
Healing is occurring.
He is mending,
slowly
but surely.
Perhaps the same is true of my heart.

Inadequacy

To know your grace suffices e'en for me
Requires that I must be
Convinced of my inadequacy.
In weakness, I am free to see
Your sov'reignty.
I fear to pay the price, but I fear too
The cost of trading true
Hope for futility. Help me to
Accept the things I cannot do
And trust in you.

Comparison, Come to Kill Again

Comparison, come to kill again, quick
To cripple, curse, cry foul, foment, and feed
Confusion till desire seems more like need.
God's grace grows grey, his manna makes me sick
Even as it sustains me. Still I stick
Stock in distinctions, hear his call but heed
Too my brother's call. He blossoms. I bleed.
Truth bids me trust. I tremble and cry, "Trick!"

Dethrone, O God, the god of my making,
Myself as ultimate, false comfort, chief
Of my affections choking out true love,
Unlovely leech of joy. Set to breaking
My false assumptions and restore belief
In your good will and all my lot thereof.

God's Grandeur Considered

As Hopkins saw, your grandeur does not pale,
Does not diminish though we sin and stain
Ourselves and earth. We work in pride and pain.
And through it all, your purposes prevail.
How can it be that we, so foul and frail,
Do not exhaust your grace? For grass and grain
And goodness still persist. You give us rain
And wrap us in provision. Though we fail
To follow, you forgive and give us love,
Your character conveyed in ev'ry sign
And ev'ry word, a freshness undefiled.
Decay, despair, and death touch not the dove
Who brings in darkness brightness so divine
And choicest comforts for the fearful child.

Past Midnight

Past midnight, pen in hand and mind awake.
I write line one but draw a blank at two,
Unsure of what to do.
Imagination bade me start to make
This brief display of words, but I must do
Some work to see it through.

Not ev'ry line is given.
Directed, but not driven.

But so it is with you.
You work in us to will and work yet do
Not call us to inaction. We must take
Our crosses, follow you,
And trust when we can't see because you do.
And you will ne'er forget, fail, nor forsake.

Change, Part One

What good are words, and what will they achieve?
For they are small before the might of hate
And faulty too: they bend beneath the weight
Of generations. Can we e'er relieve
The burdens under which our brothers heave,
All hoping against hope that soon the wait
Will end in rest, in justice, in a state
Of peace and love and welcome? Now, we grieve,
For hope remains a hope, a thing unseen,
Desire unsatisfied, dream unfulfilled.
Bring justice, Lord, grant peace, and intervene.
Convict and humble us till we are stilled.
Let tragedy not be the final scene.
Let now the hard soil of our souls be tilled.

Change, Part Two

Let now the hard soil of our souls be tilled,
And let us not resist the needed change.
Let not another be unjustly killed.
Let what is common now become most strange.
Lord, show us our responsibility
And lead us in compassion. Let the cries
For justice not end in futility
But further freedom as our pray'rs arise.
Let us be quick to listen, slow to speak,
And slow to anger with no room for sin.
Let those with power learn to live as meek,
And let this lifelong journey now begin.
Teach us to meet all souls with love and grace
As we now learn to welcome and embrace.

Change, Part Three

As we now learn to welcome and embrace,
We recognize that sin still will infect
Our hearts and homes and homelands, and we face
The difficulty, striving to connect
What oft is torn asunder, faith and works,
With faith our present work is not in vain.
We serve the one who neither shuns nor shirks
His sheep, and he will soon remove the stain
Of sin, for he in justice shall return,
And all that now is wrong he will set right.
We wait and hope, our hearts within us burn-
ing for the dawn's approach, the end of night.
All our division then will be undone,
The broken brought together by the Son.

The Savior's Song

The time-tested timbre of truth resounds
In every tragedy turned triumph,
Each near-forgotten promise come to pass,
All victories of love after a loss.

Surrounded though we are by many sounds,
Some subtle, others sharp in the circumf-
erence of our souls, still none shall surpass
The Savior's song, the echoes of the cross.

Purification

You have rent my heart. You rend it still
That I might do your will.
Continue. Kill
Whate'er contrasts you in me, makes me ill.

I am slowly learning to be still
In faith that soon you will
Finally kill
Corruption, cleanse each stain, and cure each ill.

Sadness is a growing thing

Sadness is a growing thing.
It is watered by frustrated plans,
fed by unfulfilled affections,
lengthened by loss.

Sadness is a subtle thing.
Unchecked, it soon can choke
life and love and laughter
as grief sours and
breeds bitterness.

Sadness is a frail thing.
It breaks open and spills out
unexpectedly
at the slightest touch.

Sadness is a fleeting thing,
a fading thing.
It is disarmed by a deeper truth,
held in perspective by purpose,
and will be redeemed
at the coming of the one
whose love was never lost.
He will wipe away every tear.

Who Are You?

Who are you? Majestic Maker of all
That moves and all that remains still. You fill
With fullness all spaces, unperceived, call
Dead things to life, direct with perfect will
Without removing our ability
To truly love and to be loved by you.
You are the true source of tranquility,
The good shepherd, trustworthy, steadfast through
Every scene of the story. You are
The center and the circumference, all-
Encompassing and all-surpassing, far
Beyond, nearer still. Somehow you still call
Our small souls into fellowship and free
Our idol eyes to readjust and see.

Poets

The poets worshiped you through verse and rhyme,
Turned their imaginations to the task
Of translating eternity to time
That image bearers might be taught to bask
In light refracted through a humble lens,
Refracted so to share a diff'rent view
Of beauty. Souls in wonder took up pens
And wrote to cultivate their love of you.
One wonders if the words will ever cease,
If all might soon be said, each rhyme fulfilled.
But throes of life persist, and words bring peace,
So movement of the quills will not be stilled.
Rise up, you poets, scribes of humble soul,
To teach and train us better to extol.

Redeem

How can you redeem what I have done?
I have sought solace in sin,
    worshiped idols, chose
        self over you.
True,
    you are sovereign still,
        ruler over every realm.
But how I rebel,
    rejecting life,
    desiring death.
I wound
    myself as well as
    those I love
        less than I love myself
        but more than I love you.
I have no excuse,
    no plea but your pardon,
    no hope but your help.
Salvage me
    that I might be useful,
        perhaps even
            faithful.
May it be.
    Have mercy.
        Redeem even me.

Little Sins

Subdue my unconcern with little sins,
Death in installments, small sips of decay,
Rebellions I would rather overlook.

Correct the imperfection in the lens
Through which I see and fail to see the way
I idolize the gods that I forsook.

Provision

Some hopes are dashed upon the throne of grace,
Are lifted up in pray'r to be denied.
And though it seems the Father hides his face,
We need not fear that he will not provide.
But his provision oft is of a kind
Perceived unkind while in the midst of loss.
What he deems "need" is diff'rently defined.
Sometimes the crown is traded for the cross.
But crosses borne in faith will always form
Our souls as needed, so we need not fret.
His grace suffices for the fiercest storm.
None who trust full in him shall feel regret.
But it is faith—not sight—that shows the way.
God is our shepherd. We need ne'er dismay.

Discontentment

How many days
will I dust these shelves
in this room
until I am allowed to move
and can then,
finally,
dust these same shelves
in a different room?

Denial

Whether three times,
fearful,
or seventy times seven times,
graceful,
we all will deny
one of two persons
daily.

With a Storm

How do you respond
    (w)hen t(h)e w(i)nd (s)hakes your tem(p)orary dwelling?
    when the thund(e)r b(r)eaks your sense of calm?

    (w)hen t(h)e l(i)ghtning (s)trikes your storehouses?
    when all around you is (p)urifying floodwat(e)r and fi(r)e
        life-giving,
        all-consuming?

What do you do
    when the Father answers your prayers with a storm
      and a whisper?

Do you run away?
Where else would you go?

There is a response
    when the w(i)nd sh(a)kes your te(m)porary dwelling.
    when the thunder (b)reaks your sens(e) of calm.

    when the lightning (s)trikes your storehouses.
    when all around you is purifying floodwa(t)er and f(i)re,
        (l)ife-giving,
        a(l)l-consuming.

Lost

Some of my favorite verbs became so
because of
prepositional phrases and
direct objects.
I am sad now because
those verbs have become
past tense.

I wait for you, often impatiently

I wait for you, often impatiently.
Passionate and shortsighted is my soul,
Resistant to the truth of your control.
My faith wars with my fears consistently.
I pray for grace to give up while I grip
More tightly to what you require of me,
Thinking of faith as eyes widen to see
Any way out. A trembling heart and lip
Often appear instead of steadfastness,
Longing for Egypt in the Promised Land,
Reaching for idols as you hold my hand.
Spirit, sustain me. Help me see past this.
Teach me to rest in your ability
And wait in rev'rence and humility.

Delight

When the Maker made all things good,
    it was so.

He spoke
    not flippantly but
        with purpose,
    not carelessly but
        with creativity.

Every good gift,
    every perfect gift,
        is from above.

If this is true,
    delight did not sneak in.

When the Maker made all things good,
    it was so.

Confession

Confession: I wish you would do my will,
For I would rather not surrender all.
I would prefer more say in what you call
Me to within your kingdom. Only kill
Those parts of me with which I wish to part.
Pick from the list I curate, then begin
To excise only my unwanted sin,
But leave the rest lest you disturb my heart.

O weak desire, false freedom, foolish dream.
Such service would be fiction, for the throne
Would be yours in name only. Lord, remove
Me from my central focus and redeem
All places where my heart is still like stone.
In grace and mercy, pardon and reprove.

Surrender

My hands shake,
    holding tight to any semblance of
        control.
I fear
    if I let go,
        I will be left with nothing.

But you say,
    "Seek first . . .,"
    "Deny yourself . . .,"
    "I have overcome the world."

So I let go
    and find
        my hands were always empty.

To pray and not lose heart is no small task

To pray and not lose heart is no small task,
To come before the throne without a mask,
Revealing all your deepest doubts and fears
And failures, then to still step forth and ask

For help and hope. You tremble, feeling tears
As faith, formed over long, uncertain years,
Stands face to face with yet another test
That threatens to undo you. But he hears

The weakness in your voice and offers rest.
He knows your heart is breaking, calls you blessed
And calls for faith again, promising peace
In perseverance, that his way is best.

And so you pray in hope, and you release
Control of circumstances, so to cease
From all burdensome worries and to bask
In grace before the lamb with crimson fleece.

Testing

I.
I cannot understand.
Perhaps
that is part of
the point.
Embrace the unknown.

II.
How has it come to this?
When I started, things seemed
simpler.
Now,
nothing seems sure.

III.
I cannot escape.
I cannot escape.
I cannot escape.
I cannot escape.
I cannot escape.

IV.
This is beyond my control.
I have two choices:
cling more tightly
or release my grip.
Both threaten to break me.

The Dark

Why does the dark disturb us so?
Why does the terror never go away?

What do the shadows seek to show
To those at peace who only know the day?

What do we fear that we will be
When faced with our mortality and time?

And will we meet eternity
Complete unless we learn to see the rhyme?

Stillness

Stillness scares me.

In the quiet, I can more easily
    hear you.
When I hear you,
    will you again call me to
        surrender and sacrifice?

There is no other way.
    Sometimes, though,
        I wish there was.

Have mercy, O God.

Hindsight may well make small what now looms large

Hindsight may well make small what now looms large.
Perspective minimizes life,
Fits disparate chapters into stories,
Draws from our griefs new glories.
So do not lose heart in sadder stories.
These too contribute to true life.
By grace, such tests make little faith grow large.

Lesser

I am weary,
weary from bearing the weight
of waiting
for some other weight
to be removed.

But I wear too
an easy yoke,
a light burden,
and it makes all weights
not less
but lesser.

Loss and Grace

Some things are lost never to be recovered.
Some absences are gifts shrouded in grief.
Apart from pain, some truths stay undiscovered.
Some losses point the way to true relief.
But future glory does not make less real
The sufferings we meet from day to day.
Christ does not minimize the pain we feel;
Christ knows it best and shows there is a way
For loss to pave the road to greater gain,
For suffering to serve a holy end.
We mourn in hope, for nothing is in vain
In service to the ever-faithful friend.
Count it all joy no matter what you face.
Feel deep the loss, then rest in perfect grace.

I draw near to you

With weak prayers and little faith,
with a broken and divided heart,
I draw near to you,
knowing that you, though gentle and kind,
will not suffer sin to persist
in your presence.

Waiting

The psalmist waited patiently for you
And then bore witness to your care and grace.
Relief followed the waiting like the dew
After a night when darkness hid your face.
Though you are never absent, we may not
Detect you in the time before the dawn.
Your promises—oft doubted, oft forgot—
Prove true, a hope long hidden, never gone.
But patience is required, for though the end
Is certain, yet it does not come too soon.
You use the time we wait to break and mend.
In silence, we learn how to sing in tune.

So hope, though time be now a source of strain.
Our waiting on the Lord is not in vain.

You call me to surrender

You call me to surrender,
to lay down the desires of my heart
willingly.
I would rather you take them from me,
for then my part would only be
to accept what I cannot change.
To give me a choice—
that is a difficult test.
But let me be found faithful.
Help me to trade treasure
for greater treasure,
the fleeting for the lasting,
to sit through the eclipse
by faith.
None who wait for you shall be put to shame.

8:35pm, 12/25/20

Outside, the winter's chill.
Inside, the warm light's glow.
The atmosphere is still
As Christmas carols ring,
O'erpow'ring all ill will
That often dwells below
And changing hearts until
We all begin to sing.

NOTES

All poems originally appeared on the blog asilearntowalk.com

"All to your throne" contains a reference to John Donne's poem "Batter my heart, three-person'd God."

In "Despite What Eyes Can See," the phrase "path of sorrows" was inspired by a song of the same name by All Sons and Daughters.

"Wants" includes a paraphrase of Augustine's famous line from his *Confessions*.

"God's Granduer Considered" references Gerard Manley Hopkins's poem "God's Grandeur."

"Monday Evening" was published in *The Poetry Pub Chapbook Vol. 2: 2020*. You can find that chapbook here: https://thepoetrypub.com/chapbooks

"With a Storm" would not be what it is today without the contributions of Andrew Wilson. He helped with both the structure and the content, improving the rough draft immeasurably and guiding the poem to its final form. I'm incredibly grateful for his feedback and help in the writing process of this poem.

ACKNOWLEDGMENTS

Thank you to everyone who played a role in the writing process of these poems. Whether you recommended topics, suggested edits, or offered your thoughts on the poems as they were being written, you helped to make them what they are today. I'm so thankful for you. Thank you especially to Joe Fontenot and Marilyn Stewart for their critical eyes, technical support, and consistent encouragement. Thank you also to everyone who encouraged me and affirmed me in my writing. I pray these poems serve you well.

Otherland
Books

Made in the USA
Columbia, SC
10 April 2025

56436460R00086